Ultralight Aircraft

by K. C. Kelley

Published by The Child's World®
1980 Lookout Drive
Mankato, MN 56003-1705
800-599-READ
www.childsworld.com

The Child's World®: Mary Berendes, Publishing Director
Shoreline Publishing Group, LLC: James Buckley Jr.,
    Production Director
The Design Lab: Design and production

ISBN 9781609732097
LCCN 2011940086

Photo credits: Cover: Dreamstime.com/Ian Bracegirdle.
Interior: Corbis: 7; dreamstime.com: Ian Bracegirdle
13, Mark Atkins 16, 19, Oksanaphoto 22, Babmi
Dingman 26; iStock: 11, 21, 29; Photos.com: 8, 15;
P&M Aviation: 25

Printed in the United States of America

Table of Contents

Flying with birds helped make ultralight flying popular.

CHAPTER ONE

Good for the Goose!

People have been watching birds since . . . well, since there were people. Down on the ground, people wondered, "How can I fly like the birds?"

William Lishman answered that question. Born in Canada, Lishman had loved flying since he was young. He built an **aircraft** called an ultralight. This craft mixed a small engine with wings like a hang glider. Soon he was flying alongside flocks of Canada geese. In 1993, scientists asked him to help **endangered** whooping cranes learn to **migrate**.

To help the cranes, Lishman first flew with the geese he knew so well. That year, he trained 400 geese and flew side-by-side with them across Canada. A year later, he led the first flight of cranes from Florida to their summer home in the northern Midwest. The experiment worked! Ultralights could help young birds learn to find their homes.

Today, thanks to ultralights, Operation Migration has helped thousands of birds. A movie called *Flying Home* gives a real bird's-eye view of their work. Lishman's first ultralight is on display at the Smithsonian Air & Space Museum in Washington D.C. Turns out we can fly with the birds after all!

Operation Migration leads cranes home to their nests.

What's in a Name?

These small, one-pilot craft are called ultralights in the United States and Canada. However, other countries use other names. These include ultra-lites, microlites, and trikes. If you read about "sport flying," that means very small airplanes, but doesn't really mean ultralight aircraft.

An ultralight's engine turns this large propeller to give the aircraft power.

Lishman was not the first person to fly ultralights. John Moody made the first ultralight aircraft in Wisconsin in 1975. He put an engine on the back of a wide-winged glider. Though he nearly crashed on his first flight, soon ultralights were a success. In 1982, the U.S. government created rules to make ultralights legal and safer. For instance, ultralights can only fly in daylight and away from crowded cities.

Ultralights have not only helped birds find their homes. Ultralights also give pilots a fun way to do what they love—fly. The craft are one-seat machines. They have fabric-covered wings like a glider and a small engine. Most engines are powered by gas. Some ultralights use electric motors. They all have open **cockpits**, which is where the pilot sits. Most ultralights have three wheels used in takeoff and landing.

The key to ultralights is that they can fly much slower than airplanes. Pilots can really look down and see what's below them. In airplanes, they're moving much too fast to really sight-see. That slow speed is also what makes the work of pilots like William Lishman possible. The ultralights can slow down to match the birds' speed. Ultralights can also change directions more quickly than planes.

Plus, the open cockpit also gives pilots a great feeling of the wind in their face. For people who love flying, ultralights are ultra-adventure!

This pilot has fired up the engine and is heading toward takeoff.

A two-person ultralight is used for training new pilots.

CHAPTER TWO

Ultralight Basics

You don't have to be an official pilot to fly an ultralight. In fact, some teenagers have learned to fly them. You don't need a **license**, but you do need training. Ultralight flyers first take classroom lessons. They learn about air safety, weather, and **navigation** (which means finding where you want to go using maps). They learn all the controls of the ultralight. In a special two-seat craft, students fly with teachers. They learn by actually flying the ultralight. The teacher is there to show them how.

Pilots also need an ultralight. A new ultralight can cost nearly $10,000. Used ultralights can be found for less.

People who love ultralights love aircraft of all sorts. Some pilots actually build their own ultralights. They can use a kit that comes with all the parts. Creative people can create their own parts and designs as well.

Though you don't need a license, your aircraft might. Local air officials can check the craft for safety. They make sure that all the parts work correctly and that pilots have the right gear. For instance, ultralight pilots should have a two-way radio. They use it to speak with people on the ground.

Ultralights take people many places regular airplanes can't land. And that doesn't just mean actual land. Some ultralights can land on water. Instead of wheels, they use large "pods" that float. Other ultralights use skis to land on ice or snow.

Ultralight wings are fabric stretched over an aluminum frame.

Ultralight pilots always take off into the wind.

In an emergency, the pilot probably can't use a parachute. It would be too hard to climb out of the ultralight in the air. However, the ultralight itself can have a parachute. If there is trouble, the pilot can pull a cord. A chute will pop out of a box above the wings. The entire ultralight, pilot and all, can float safely to the ground. Pilots also should wear helmets in case of rough landings. Goggles are also important to keep the eyes clear in the wind.

Once you have the ultralight and the training, you're ready to fly. After checking the weather and all the gear (don't forget gas for the engine!), a pilot is ready to fly. He points the ultralight into the wind. After starting the engine, he releases the wheel brake. The propeller churns faster and faster. As the craft reaches speed, the pilot pulls back on the stick . . . and up he goes!

The first ultralights were steered by shifting the pilot's weight. They acted much like a hang glider. To tilt left or right, the pilot slid his body in a **harness**. To move up or down, the pilot pushed or pulled a lever that raised or lowered the front of the wing.

Today's ultralights are more like airplanes. They have instrument panels that show altitude (height above the ground) and speed in the air. Once he's in the air, the pilot uses a control stick to turn left or right. With foot pedals, he makes the ultralight head down or up.

Pilots can look past their controls for an awesome view of the land below.

To land, pilots slowly bring their ultralight toward a long, flat spot like this beach.

After the flight, it's time to land. The ultralight pilot aims for his landing spot. He sinks toward the ground with the spot far in front of him. As he gets near to the ground, he reduces speed. After the wheels touch down smoothly, he uses brakes to stop the aircraft.

Another successful flight is over . . . time to gas up for another one!

CHAPTER THREE

Stories from the Sky

What's good for the goose is also good for the whooping crane. The whooping cranes that Operation Migration lead across the United States are starting to grow in numbers. Other ultralights now help sandhill cranes learn to migrate as well.

Helping birds is not the only way ultralight pilots get in their flights. Pilots compete at events that test their landing skills or speed. Other events challenge how well they navigate. In a cross-country race, pilots must take off and land at checkpoints on a course. The pilot who completes the entire course fastest and with good landings is the winner.

A slow flight over this field of flowers makes for a pretty picture.

In a two-person event, the co-pilot sits in back and helps with maps and directions.

At the World Championships, top ultralight pilots gather to see who is the best. The most recent event was held in 2009 in the Czech [pronounced CHECK] Republic. A pair of British flyers, Robert Grimwood and Chris Saysell, took home the top prize. At this event, the pilots had to zoom around an obstacle course marked by enormous cones. The 2011 World Championships will be held in Israel.

Other ultralight flyers aim for world records. In 1989, Eric Scott-Winton flew higher than any other pilot. He took his aircraft 30,000 feet (9,144 m) above an airport in his native Australia. In 1988, a Belgian pilot set the record for longest flight in a straight line. Bernard d'Otreppe zoomed 4,491 feet (1,369 km) through France.

Aircraft similar to ultralights are powered paragliders. These craft have engines, but the flyers hang below a wide **canopy** like a parachute. Though they can't go as high, these flyers can do amazing acrobatic tricks. Mathieu Rouanet of France is one of the world's most famous paragliders. He travels the world giving shows and competing. He has won four World Championships in this high-flying sport.

A parasail with a motor has created a new type of aircraft.

Spectacular views await ultralight and paragliding pilots.

The world record for altitude by a paraglider was set in 2008. Ramon Morillas Salmeron of Spain flew 22,050 feet (6,721 m) above the Canary Islands.

Ultralights and powered paragliders continue to amaze people on the ground below. The pilots of these craft look down and know that they have the answer. They know what it's like to fly like a bird.

Glossary

aircraft—any type of machine that flies

canopy—a wide fabric cover over something

cockpit—the seating area in an aircraft

endangered—for wildlife, in danger of disappearing from the earth

harness—straps and fasteners that connect a person to something

license—an official document that gives permission to do something

migrate—to travel back and forth on a regular schedule

navigation—finding your way using maps and other means

Find Out More

BOOKS

Eyewitness: Flying Machine
By Andrew Nahum (DK Children, 2004)
A photo-packed guide to everything that flies with help from a motor or an engine—from ultralights to supersonic jets.

Saving the Whooping Crane
By Susan Goodman (Millbrook Press, 2007)
Fly along with the people (and birds) of Operation Migration as they help whooping cranes by using ultralights.

Ultralights
By Joanne Mattern (Rourke Publishing, 2009)
More information about how to fly these unique aircraft.

WEB SITES

For links to learn more about extreme sports: **childsworld.com/links**

Note to Parents, Teachers, and Librarians: We routinely verify our Web links to make sure they are safe and active sites. So encourage your readers to check them out!

Index

About the Author

K.C. Kelley is happier in big airplanes than he would be in ultralights! Back on the ground, he enjoys writing books for young readers. He has written about baseball, football, and soccer, as well as about animals, astronauts, and other cool stuff.